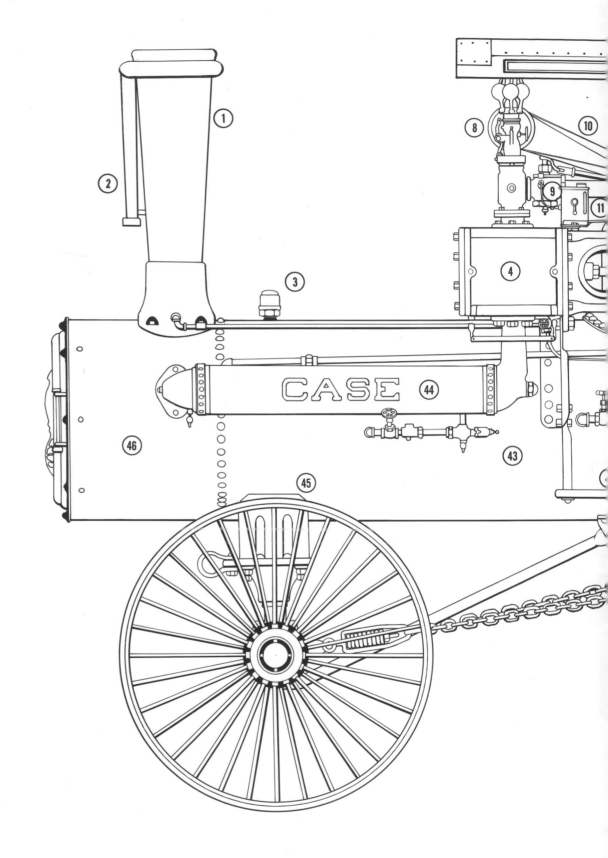

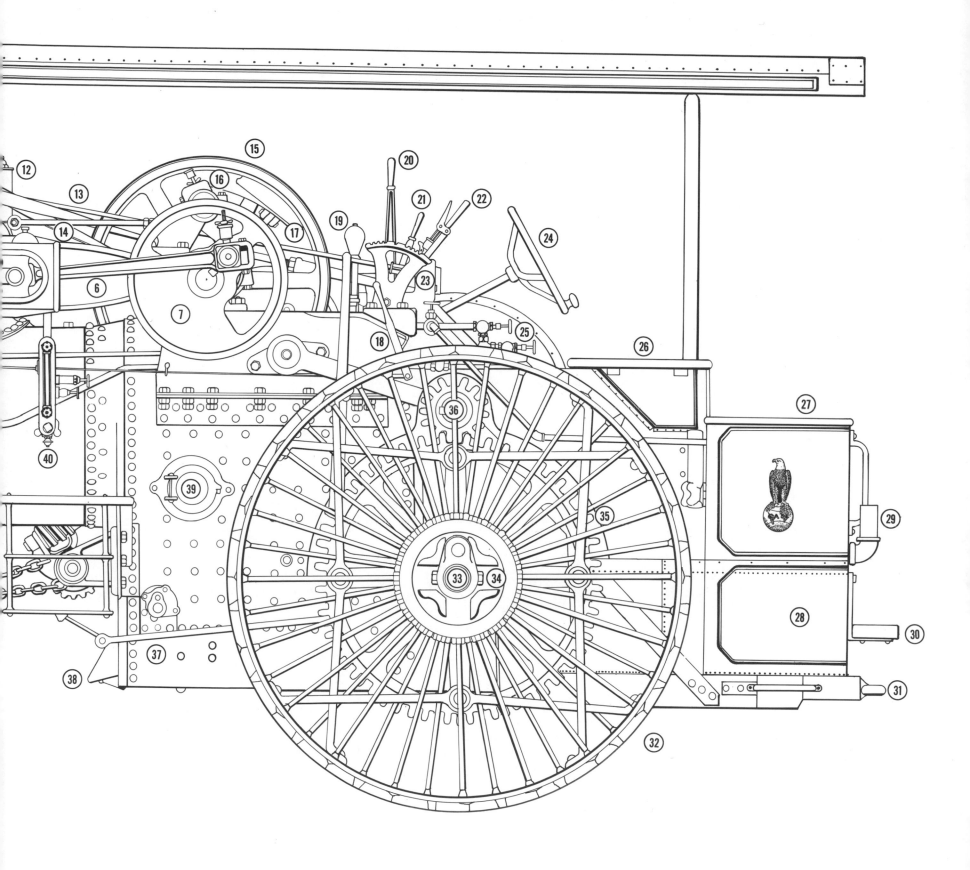

THRASHIN' TIME

THRASHIN'

HARVEST DAYS IN

TIME

THE DAKOTAS

by David Weitzman

DAVID R. GODINE, PUBLISHER • BOSTON

First published in 1991 by
DAVID R. GODINE, PUBLISHER, INC.
Post Office Box 450
Jaffrey, New Hampshire 03452
www.godine.com

LIBRARY OF CONGRESS CATALOGING-IN-PUBLICATION DATA
Weitzman, David L.
Thrashin' Time / by David Weitzman. — 1st ed.
p.   cm.
Summary: A young boy describes his life on a family farm in North Dakota
in the early part of the twentieth century, particularly the arrival
of a new steam-powered threshing machine.
ISBN 1-56792-110-8 (softcover)
[1. Farm life — Fiction. 2. Threshing machines — Fiction.
3. North Dakota — Fiction. 4. Great Plains — Fiction.] I. Title.
PZ7.W448184TH   1991
[FIC] — dc20   91-55524 CIP AC

First softcover printing, January 2000
PRINTED IN CANADA

For my daughter, Arin

Within the circles of our lives
We dance the circles of the years,
the circle of the seasons.

—Wendell Berry, THE WHEEL

Contents

·I·

Steam Power

P<small>A SAYS</small> the engine has the strength of sixty-five horses and the smoke from the stack can be seen for miles around. He says the engine gets the separator going so fast that the four of us will be doing all we can do just to keep up with it. That it will thrash more wheat in a day than you could imagine. "You'll have to be fast on the handle to feed one of those."

I saw a steam engine thrashin' wheat once, last year. Pa and Ma and Anna, my little sister, and I were out in the field piling the sheaves up in shocks, when I happened to look up. "Hey, look over west." Puffs of black smoke dusted the sky. Ma dropped the bundle she was stacking. "Oh, Gabe, it's a prairie fire!" Pa shielded his eyes against the noon sun and squinted at the smoke. "Naw, that's no fire, Maggie. See how the smoke's a-jumpin' up in the air like that? Looks to me like they've one of those new steam engines workin' over at the Solheims'." Steam engine! I couldn't imagine such a thing on a farm.

Anna and I began pestering Pa to take us over to see the new engine. But it didn't take much doing. I could tell he wanted to go as much as we did. Pa glanced again at the smoke billowing into the sky. "Ya, sure,

we can go. I'll finish up a bit here. Peter, you go hitch the horses up to the wagon. Maggie, if you and Anna put up a picnic, we'll go have us a look at that steam engine."

We got there to find that a lot of folks had come in wagons and buggies to gather 'round and watch the thrashin'. Steam engines were still new in these parts. And there it was, the engine with its dark blue boiler, shiny brass whistle, red wheels all decorated with yellow stripes, gears spinning and rods going back and forth, rocking gently in time to the puffs of smoke from the stack—*tucka-tucka-tucka-tucka-tucka*. The sounds, that's what I liked. *Tucka-tucka-tucka-tucka* and the little steam engine going *ss—ss—ss—ss—ss—ss—ss*. The engine was quieter than I thought it would be. It was almost alive like the horses working everywhere 'round it. And the horses. Why, I'll betcha there were sixty head, big horses—Belgians and Percherons—coming and going that afternoon. Teams pulled bundle wagons heaped tall with sheaves of wheat in from the fields, pulled wagons of yellow grain away from the separator to the silo. Another team hauled the water wagon, and another wagon brought loads of cord wood to keep the engine running sunup to sundown.

It was like the Fourth of July. Kids clambered up and slid down the hay stacks, played tag and skip-to-my-lou. Some of the men were pitching horseshoes and you could hear the thump of shoes fallen too short and the solid clank of a ringer. The women looked after all the little kids and put out lunches on big tables—heaps of potato salad, sandwiches, cakes and cookies and frosty pitchers of iced tea. Dogs napped in the dark cool under the wagons, not paying any mind to the puppies tumbling all over them. The older boys stood around together, pretending they were chewing plugs of tobacco, hawking and spitting, like the thrashermen, only theirs wouldn't come brown. The men stood around the engine and the separator, puffing on their pipes, thumbs hooked under their suspenders. They inspected every part of that machine, pointing to this and that, looked up and down the belt stretching between the engine and separator in a long figure eight. Most of them had never seen a steam traction engine before.

Some of the older folks didn't like the new machine. "The old ways is the best ways," one of them said, tugging on his whiskers. "All this talk about steam engines is just a bunch of gibble-gabble," agreed another, "I'll stick to my oxen and horses." Others told of hearing all about engines exploding, killing and maiming the thrashin' crews, of careless engineers starting fires that burned up the farmer's whole crop and his barn besides. "Horses live off the land," Mr. Bauer said, "and don't need wood nor coal. No, nothin' but some hay and oats and we don't have to buy that! What's more they give you foals." He reached over and rubbed his hand down the neck of a stout gray Percheron mare hitched to a grain wagon. "All you get from steam engines is debt." Mr. Bjork agreed, "and what would we do for fertilizer? Steam engines don't make much manure, you know." Everyone laughed. "More trouble than they're worth. Why, last year Silas McGregor had to come borrow my oxen to pull his engine out of the mud. Wouldn't have one of those smoke-snortin' strawburners on my place," old Mr. Erstad scoffed, turning and waving away the scene.

But Mr. Torgrimson, now I could tell he was enjoying it. We were looking at the steam engine there up on the boiler, the connecting rod whizzing back and forth and the flywheel spinning so that the spokes were just a red blur. He was smiling and his eyes just twinkled. Then he pointed the stem of his pipe at the engine, squinted in a thoughtful way and rocked back and forth on his heels. "You know, Peter, that's a wonderful thing, the steam engine. You're witnessin' the beginnin's of real scientific farmin'." He couldn't take his eyes off that engine. "I read about a steam outfit—over Casselton way it was—that thrashed more than six thousand bushels in one day! Imagine that, six thousand bushels in just one day! Why you and your Ma and Pa all workin' together couldn't do more'n twenty or thirty in the same time."

Mr. Torgrimson was the one who told me all about bonanza farming, where a bunch of engines would start out together, side-by-side, before daybreak, each pulling a fourteen-bottom plow almost as wide as our house. "They go all day, Peter, breakin' up thousands of acres of prairie grasslands before they rest at night—some even have head lamps so they can just keep going all night. The holdin's are so big, young fellow, that they go on 'n on for days like that 'fore they reach their line and turn 'round and plow back to where they started. Day after day, week after week they go up and back. Then they sowed all that land to wheat and thrashed one hundred and sixty-two thousand—here, I'll just write that number in the dust so you can see how big it is—162,000 bushels of wheat that season."

I could tell Pa liked the engine too. He got up on the wagon and pitched bundles for a while, and then stood on the engine platform talking to the engineer, Mr. Parker. When he got down, he came over and put his hand on my shoulder, all the time looking at that engine, shaking his head like he couldn't believe his eyes. "Parker's got some machine there, by jippers, quite an outfit. What do you think about all this, Peter, steam power instead of horse power?"

I wasn't sure. "If the engine took the place of the horses, I think I'd miss Annie and Lulu and Quinn. Wouldn't you, Pa?"

"I would, but, you know, horse-power thrashin' is awful hard on them, son. Sure, I'd miss them, but we work them hard all year plowin', and diskin', and seedin' and mowin'. Then just when they're so tuckered out, about to drop and needin' a good rest, we put them to thrashin'. You and I both have seen too many good horses broken, seen them drop, die of the heat and tiredness right there in the traces. And for all their work we might get a hundred bushels, maybe two in a day. I don't know, Peter, maybe steam power is a better thing. I just don't know." Pa chuckled and his eyes got all crinkled and wrinkled with laugh lines the way they do. "I do know one thing though. If you asked the horses, I betcha they wouldn't be against this new steam power the way some folks 'round here are."

From then on Pa talked a lot about steam engines. And I began reading the stories in *The American Thresherman* about steam power. There are pages of advertisements for engines and separators—Minneapolis, J. I. Case, Advance, Nichols & Shepard. They'd been there all along, of course, but I hadn't noticed them before. It's a special day when *The American Thresherman* appears in the mailbox. I turn right to the "Boys and Girls" page. There are always folk tales like "How Friend Deer Mouse Outwitted Old Tiger," puzzles, poems, and stories with lots of facts in them telling how pencils are made or how to raise calves and piglets. There are recipes for making fudge and chocolate crisps and candied popcorn. And I read to Anna the letters from kids all over the country to "Aunt Jane," telling all about their lives.

Once I helped Anna write a letter to "Aunt Jane." We began her letter like the other kids' letters—"Dear Aunt Jane, may I join your merrie circle?" And then Anna went on to tell about how she's six now, a big girl, and old enough to run the milk separator each morning after

her brother—that's me—and her father milk the two cows, Daisy and Polly. She told how she feeds the chickens, gathers eggs, and curries the horses too. Well, what do you know, two or three months later, there was Anna's letter printed right there on the "Boys and Girls" page. And Anna was so excited she took it to school to show our teacher, Miss Stavens.

But now I like to read about steam thrashin', sometimes with Ma and Pa reading out loud. Usually, Pa hasn't much time to read with me until winter, so we catch up on our reading on long nights with the kerosene lamp turned up bright and the wind howling outside. I like the part each month called "The Threshers' School of Modern Methods," where you read about how to fire and run a steam engine, or set the blower just right so you don't lose too much grain in the straw. One month it showed how to stitch belt ends together. Another told you how to decide if a bridge was safe. That's a real problem, it says. Most of our bridges were built for horses and wagons or, at most, a yoke of oxen—two or three tons all told. But steam engines, now, they're different. They can weigh twelve tons! Imagine that. Then, put behind the engine the separator, and the water tank, and a wood or coal wagon and you've got a lot of weight on an old bridge. In almost every issue there's a picture of an engine fallen through a bridge down into a ravine or river below. Sometimes the engineer and fireman are crushed or scalded to death by steam from the broken boiler. Pa says that if we're going to have a steam engine on our place, we'll have to fix up the little timber bridge down at the end of our road.

What would that be like, having a steam engine that thrashes wheat and plows besides, right here on our place? All my life—all twelve years of it—we've treaded out the wheat the way Pa and his folks have always done. In the spring, Pa breaks the land with a walking plow pulled by Lulu or Quinn. When it's time to harvest, he hitches the horses up to the mower. And then we—all of us, Ma and Anna too—gather up the grain in bundles, tie it and stack it in shocks, head to head, pointing to the sky.

A couple of weeks later, after the wheat's had a chance to sweat under the hot sun, we stack it on wagons and haul it to our barn. Pa scrapes off a big ring on the ground, leaving it hard-packed and clean. Then we spread the wheat straw out all around the ring. The thrashin' begins when Pa leads Lulu and Percy with a halter to the circle, then he stands in the middle and starts them around. The grain is tramped out by the horses' hooves as they go around and around. Pa stops the horses after the first few times around, so we can draw off the long straw. Then he gets them going around and around again until he knows all the grain has been treaded off the straw. We pick up the straw and Ma rakes up the kernels of grain and scoops them up into bushel baskets.

We don't do the whole crop at one time. Pa stores some of the wheat in the barn and we thrash it as we need it. In the dead of winter, with snow blowing and drifting all around and the temperature to where it freezes your ears in less time than it takes to do your chores, we thrash on the barn floor. It gets so cold then that if I take a glass of water up to my room with me when I go to bed it's solid ice by morning. At times the snow gets to blowing so hard that to find our way from the house to the barn we have to hold on to Pa's coattails and all feel our way along the fence.

But inside the barn is all lit up with kerosene lamps and we soon get warm, Lulu and Quinn and all of us working so hard. We all take off our coats and sweaters and soon we're sweating like it was August. Ma puts Anna up on Percy's broad back and lets her ride around and around, giggling all the time. Once, when Pa wasn't looking, I punched Percy with the fork handle and he giddapped with Anna just flapping on his back. Pa whoaed him to a stop quick enough, but Anna cried and cried and wouldn't get back on the horses that day. Percy was just in his first winter then, but Pa said he thought Percy must already weigh half a ton or better.

Pa says the new engine will change all that and we'll thrash all our wheat at once. I asked Pa how we'd get this steam traction engine and separator. He said he couldn't buy it. It costs too much money for a farmer to buy. But Mr. Parker had one and he will be traveling around the county with his custom outfit thrashin' all of our neighbors' fields—the Knutsons', the Hansons', the Skjelles', the Torgrimsons', the Siguards', the Haugens' and the others—all in their turn. Pa had joined up with the others in a thrashin' ring, he called it. "We'll all go over to thrash Pastor Swenson first, and then they'll all be comin' here with their families, all of us helpin' one another. After they're done here then we'll end at the Estrems', 'fore the snow starts flyin', I hope. What with Mr. Parker's crew and all the neighbors, there'll be a lot of folks 'round here for a few days."

Pa showed me the papers he and our neighbors signed, "Bylaws of the Crystal Springs Threshing Company." Everyone agrees to elect officers and a secretary who keeps track of the number of bushels thrashed at each place. We all agree to pay twenty-five cents for every hundred bushels thrashed. The rest is about business stuff, but at the very end there's an Article Eight, which I especially liked—"Members shall provide for a good ice cream social or watermelon carving at the close of each season's threshing."

Oh, my legs and the crick in my back. This morning when I woke up I couldn't just jump out of bed the usual way. Pa knew we had worked hard yesterday, so his first call was kind of gentle. His second call was a bit more "hurry up." I couldn't move because every muscle hurt so bad. But his third call sounded more like we'd better get a move-on. So I rolled out of bed, down on my hands and knees and stood up holding onto the chair. It took much longer to get dressed too. I guess I'll have to go easier today.

Yesterday was the first day we stacked bundles. The shocks have been sweating long enough—it's been about two weeks since we mowed. And so now it was time to stack them for thrashin'. We were up especially early, when it was still dark. I grabbed a biscuit off the stove and ran out to the barn to get my pitchfork. Pa and my cousin Ole were hitching the horses to the wagon just as the sun came up. And Pa noticed there were big thunderheads on the horizon. "Looks like maybe we'll have some rain today. Peter, you and Ole better put a little hustle in your knees."

So we set to working. Anna drove the horses and Ole and I pitched bundles up on the wagon. Lulu and Quinn take some hard pulling on the reins, but today they must've known it was little Anna up there on the seat. They were just as gentle as they could be, following along at just the right pace beside us. All the time Anna's "geeing" and "hawing" the horses, the way she's heard Pa do. Before we knew it, Ma brought our breakfast and it was six o'clock.

The mornings have turned frosty again. The earth feels cooler under bare feet now, and this morning there was ice on the water in the trough. It seems like only yesterday that it was spring, when the air turned warm and the chill was gone from milking and morning chores.

I'll always remember last spring. April's when it happened. The robins were back and we watched a mother possum carry her babies out of the barn to the little wood by the spring house. The days got longer, and we went to bed while it was still light out. Well, sometime in the middle of the night I woke up—but not all the way—to all kinds of comings and goings, up and down the stairs, lantern light in the hallway, low, whispering voices, the banging of the screen door, the squeaking of the pump and then water splashing into the kitchen sink. Later, I stumbled still sleepy down to the kitchen to dress by the warm stove. Ma gave me a bowl of oatmeal with cream and molasses, and then she looked at me with a smile that always means I'm in for a surprise. "Your Pa's out in the barn with the horses, Peter. Why don't you go see what he's up to."

Well, there was a surprise in the barn, you betcha. Tucked in close to Lulu on a soft bed of hay was a new black colt. So that's what all the noise had been about last night! Lulu licked the white blaze on the colt's forehead as he lay asleep in the light of the lantern. I went back to the house, got little Anna and carried her down to see too. We watched him stand up, all wobbly on his long legs. Anna spent most of the day in the stall, touching Percy all over, falling asleep every so often in the warm straw, watching the little colt come alive.

We decided to name him Percy, after another Percy, an old man who came to us to work on our place years ago, when Anna and I were just pups. We don't know much about that Percy, where he came from and all. Like the rest of the crew he starts somewhere in Texas or Oklahoma and follows the ripening wheat north through Kansas and Nebraska to the Dakotas. Pa said all kinds of men travel with the thrashin' crews—

tramps, factory workers, teachers, college students, store clerks, preachers, immigrants, and a barber who gave me my first real grownup haircut. Usually they'd stay together for the thrashin' season. Percy would work his way up into Canada until, when it got just too cold and the snow began to fly, he and the rest of the crew would head south again, toward the sun. He told us once how he knew it was time to leave—"when the snow's eight inches deep and the ponds are froze over. Why it once snowed so hard up there in Moose Jaw that it took three men and a boy to hold a blanket over the keyhole just so's the room wouldn't fill up with snow."

I guess you'd call Percy a hobo. He spends much of his life going from place to place riding in, or under, or on top of boxcars. And he doesn't seem to have a last name—many of the men don't. "I'm just an old bindlestiff," he said once, "ridin' the rods, goin' wherever those long steel rails will take me." Pa heard tell that Percy was running from something, that he had got himself into some kind of trouble trying to get workers to join a union—the Wobblies, Pa called them. But Pa didn't care. "He's as good and honest a worker as we've ever had on this place and that's all I care to know about him."

Percy likes us kids, which is why he's been coming to work on our place all these years now. Once he brought me a peach of a jackknife— I carry it with me all the time—with two blades and an awl that fold out of its real bone handle. He brought Anna a little Indian doll he called a Kachina that he got way out in Arizona. He said the Hopi people make these dolls for their children to help them learn the stories of their people.

Percy was given a harmonica a long time ago as pay for some work he did, and he would play it and sing for us in the evening after supper.

We'd be stuffed with biscuits, and potatoes and pot roast, and rhubarb pie, our bellies tight under our belts, lying up against a stack. And he'd play us songs he picked up along the way, like "Old Susanna" and another that seemed to be about Percy—

> *Going to Atlanta just to look around.*
> *Then, if things don't suit me, I'll find another town.*

And he always seemed sad when we sang the last verse, Percy, and Anna and me . . .

> *See that train a-coming, coming 'round the bend;*
> *Goodbye, little darling, I'm on my way again.*

Percy'd tell stories until we fell asleep right there under the stars. Once we sat watching the fireflies, and Anna asked Percy what they were. "Certain flies," he told us, "carry tiny lanterns, so small that we just see them as a twinkle of light. Well, the light from their lanterns helps elves and fairies find their way through the fields and woods after sundown." We woke up all wrapped up warm in Percy's bedroll while he lay snoring and curled up tight against the night chill.

When the crew showed up last fall, Percy wasn't with them. No one knew what happened to him. We all felt a sadness around his place up on the seat of the bundle wagon. Most of all, we missed the cheerful music, and the stories and the way Percy always brushed his big, gray mustache to the corners of his mouth with the back of his hand so as to get his harmonica to his lips. I'm sure hoping he comes this thrashin' season. And Pa says that could be day after tomorrow.

If so, tomorrow will be our last day of school for a while. Ma told us just as we were leaving this morning to tell our teacher that we'd be thrashin' the next few days and that Anna and I would be needed. Of course, Miss Stavens expected this. Each day in the fall, one or two of the seats would be empty. Then she would announce, "Carl and Katrina are not here. I guess the threshers have arrived at the Anders' place."

Just think, two—maybe three—whole days without Roman numerals and having to learn every jot and tittle of the grammar lesson. And arithmetic. What I don't understand is why a boy who wants to be a thrasherman and have his own rig someday needs to know how to read Roman numerals. And fractions. Who wants $\frac{1}{37}$ of anything? And why would a thrasherman need to multiply $\frac{13}{157}$ by $\frac{64}{87}$? Pa doesn't answer when I ask him except to say that learning is important and to do as the teacher tells us.

Of course Miss Stavens called on me today to recite my geography lesson. And I was prepared. North Dakota is the thirty-ninth state, Bismarck is the capital, and Fargo is the largest city. North Dakota's rivers are the Missouri and the Red River that separates it from Minnesota. To the north of our state are the Canadian provinces of Saskatchewan—I don't know how to spell that yet—and Manitoba. To the west is Montana and to the south, South Dakota.

2

Tankee

TODAY IS the day the thrashers are coming. Pa is sure they'd be through thrashin' the Haugens' place this morning and will be to our place by midday. So he's up long before daybreak and down in the kitchen before he's even dressed. Lying in the dark, I can hear him scratch a match on the stove and light the fire he laid last night. Already there are two big kettles of water on the back of the stove to be heated. *Squeak, squeak, squeak,* Pa works the pump handle up and down till water gushes into the coffeepot. He sets it down on the stove with a clank, and climbs back upstairs. I'm awake now, thinking already about the fresh donuts in the pantry and about getting up. We need to be done with milking and tending to the animals by five o'clock if we're to have everything ready for the thrashers.

It's dark when we walk out to the barn, and the stars are so bright that Anna reaches her arms up over her head and wiggles her fingers trying to touch them. It's frosty! And as we wrestle the heavy barn door open, our breath comes in steamy clouds. When I grab the milking pail off the peg the bail stings my hands with cold. I milk leaning close to Bessie, resting my forehead on her warm, furry belly. The milk rising in the pail warms my legs wrapped around and I'm thinking of a bowl of steaming hot oatmeal by the hot cook stove.

Ma and Aunt Mavis were up earlier too. The clattering of pots and pans and lids means the cooking for the day, for dozens of hungry workers, has begun. Ma was a school teacher before she and Pa were married, so she's good at getting us all working together. My cousin Ole and I lift the big pork roast into the roasting pan, and then slide it into the oven.

With a wipe of her hands on her apron, Ma turns to the next chore, making the desserts, helping Anna measure out everything—including just the right amount of baking soda to make the biscuits rise. Together they stir up the cake batter, pour it into the pans and get them into the oven. We'll have lots of good desserts while the thrashers are here, sour-cream cakes, berries and whipped cream, and pudding—lots of pudding—johnny cakes, donuts, and cookies. For days the kitchen will smell of warm yeasty dough and cinnamon and cloves.

This morning Ma gives Anna, me, and Ole special jobs. She gives Anna a small oval mirror in an old gilded frame, a hammer, and a nail and sends her out to the big elm. Anna taps a nail into the tree and hangs up the mirror for the thrashers to comb their hair and shave in. Ma notices though that the mirror's Anna's height, about four feet off the ground, and allows that the crew probably don't want to comb their hair down on their hands and knees. Anna and Ma laugh together at the notion of the big men all crawling around on the ground to look into the mirror, and Anna climbs up on a stool this time to hang it.

"Just as well if they get here later this mornin'," Pa said, coming in from the field. "We'd have to wait anyway for the dew to dry off." We're not sure when they'll arrive, so I've been keeping one eye on the end of the road. I guess I'm pretty excited. Ma says I've been jumpy as a chipmunk's nose all morning.

Tooot tooot. "It's the engine! Ma, they're here, the thrashers are here," Anna calls from the kitchen porch. We can't see the engine yet, but, sure enough, there's a dark smudge of smoke above the windbreak and a cloud of white steam jumps up into the sky just before each sharp bark of the whistle. Well, I can't wait, and run down the road to meet the engine. Ma and Aunt Mavis hurry back into the kitchen to fetch plates and pots of coffee and fresh cream. Then they carry out a big pan full of donuts and coffee cake. We'll have a little lunch for the thrashers while they're fixing to start up.

The engine steams right toward me, *chuff, chuff, chuff, chuffing* in a cloud of smoke and dust. Some of our neighbors sit on top of the separator, rumbling in tow behind the engine. Others ride in the wagons. Peter and Milly Shamburg are here, Louie and Thorwald Satcher come from the other side, and Osten Mikkel, too. Some are on horseback. Uncle Arne's here, too, driving the water wagon. I run out to the engine and then walk alongside. The engine moves so slowly that even a kid can keep up easy, and I can watch the engineer up on his platform moving levers back and forth, pulling on the whistle cord, looking out over the front of the big engine and then to each side to make sure he'll get through the gate all right.

The big J. I. Case engine lumbers into the yard. Everywhere now there's a hustle. The cats sunning on the popple-rail fence startle, look around with wide eyes and leap from every direction in flashes of orange and white and gray stripes and dive under the porch. Chickens scatter every which way. The ganders charge the engine, necks stretched out, heads low to the ground, beaks gaping, *hissssssing* at the noisy giant in

their yard. Then they turn and with wings a-flapping half run and half fly back toward the barn.

By jippers, the wheels are big, bigger than I remembered. And the stack—Mr. Parker taught me that word the first time he heard me call it the chimney—reaches into the sky. The engineer bobs up and down as he cranks the steering wheel, first one way then back round the other, heading the engine out toward the stacks in the field. I guess Mr. Parker must've seen me skipping alongside. He turns from his levers and wheel just for a moment, kneels down, and reaches out his hand to pull me up onto the step and the platform and up again behind him on the seat board.

We rumble along high up off the ground, one of Mr. Parker's gloved hands on the wheel, the other on the throttle lever. The heat off the firebox is hotter than the noon sun. When I look back, there's the separator following close behind us, and down below is Pa, looking up at me in the engine. I wave to Ma on the front porch. She waves back smiling, sort of, touching the finger tips of one hand to her mouth the way she does when she's worried. Aunt Mavis waves too, but she's laughing and looking like she really wants to be up here on the engine too.

The smells around us on the platform are wood smoke and hot oily smells. And in front of us is a gray blur of spinning wheels and shafts, stroking rods, belts, whirring gears and a brass whistle so shiny we can see our faces in it. On top of the boiler is a round brass case with a white face and numbers and a pointer that reminds me of our school clock. "That's the steam gauge," Mr. Parker explains, "it tells me how much steam pressure there is in the boiler."

Mr. Parker pushes one lever and pulls another and the engine rolls to a stop. He and Pa talk a short while about where to put the separator, whether there is still plenty of water at the pump and that they'd be having some lunch before they started in thrashin'. Mr. Parker pulls open the firebox door and looks inside, and I can feel the heat right through my britches legs. "Peter, give me a couple sticks of wood out of the bunker there and we'll get us a little more steam." He throws the wood onto the bed of orange-hot coals and then closes the firebox with a loud clang. "Now, let's get this crew to workin'."

With a lurch and a *hiss——hiss——hiss—hiss–hiss* of steam, the engine starts out toward the bundle wagons. We pull the separator over by the stacks. Mr. Parker spins the wheel first one way and then around the other till we've made a big circle and come round to face the separator. "This looks 'bout right." Mr. Parker brings the engine to where his eye tells him is just the right distance. Then, squinting along the edge and over the top of the big fly wheel, working the engine back and forth, he gets it lined up with the pulley on the separator. The wheel and the pulley have to be lined up just right or the belt won't stay on. "By jippers, Peter, I think she's in line. Now you get down there and learn about beltin' up."

When I get down I notice for the first time who all is here. I look into the faces of the men. There are young and old faces, pale and sunbrowned, Negroes, Mexicans, and Indians. I'm really looking for one face though, for a scraggly whiskered face that's Percy's, but I don't see him. I haven't heard his big voice this morning. Oh, how I hope he's come this year with more stories and harmonica tunes. He's just got to be here somewhere. Maybe he didn't recognize me up there on the engine, more grown up than he remembers. Still, it isn't his way. He always comes looking for us kids first thing . . .

"Hey, come give us a hand here!"

Mr. Haugen and Mr. Mohn have unrolled the long leather belt and stretched it out on the ground between the separator and the engine. Then they shoulder one end up onto the fly wheel. I wonder out loud how the belt stays on the fly wheel when it's turning so fast. Mr. Mohn shows me by putting my hand on the wheel how it's not really flat, but curved. This crown, he called it, is enough to keep the belt from slipping off. "And it'll always run better if you remember to put the hair side— that's the rougher side—of the leather next to the pulley." My job now is to pull the other end of the belt to the separator, put a twist in it to make a long figure eight, and help get it up on the pulley. That done, we signal Mr. Parker and he backs up the engine. The long belt jumps up off the ground, tightens, twists one way and then the other and sags just a bit, the way it works best.

"Peter! Peter, where are you?" Aw shucks! It's Aunt Mavis calling me back to the kitchen.

"Peter, I need you to fork up some potatoes, enough for supper and the next few days." It's hard to believe how many potatoes a crowd of hungry thrashers can eat. "Be sure to find a nice cool, dark place in the barn to store them." You just can't have too many potatoes, certainly not. Ma boils 'em for supper. Any left over will get fried up for breakfast tomorrow or made into potato salad for dinner. "And when you've got the potatoes put away don't be goin' off playin'. I'll need you to pick corn. We'll cook the kettle full today."

Sometimes I think more work goes into the cooking than the thrashin'. My, how those folks can eat. Ma says she never saw a man who couldn't eat five times a day, with lunch besides, especially the first day of thrashin'. Pa always calls the thrashers "chicken-and-pie outfits." And when I really eat a lot, Ma always says I must be "starving like a thrasherman who's missed his breakfast."

There's so much to do. Aunt Mavis came in from Fargo to stay with us and help out. Annie Tuerberg, Margit Rank, and Lottie Hanson came along with the crew to help. Ma gives all of us our chores. Any boys who aren't out in the field are put to work in the kitchen, work like carrying in bags of flour. They're heavy for us boys—a hundred pounds—and we're barely able to sag up the stairs with the bags. So we're always falling all over ourselves and the big limp bags of flour and wrestling, and then getting all heezed up with laughing so Ma has to come get us to working again. "You boys are as shifty as a puppy's tail. It will behoove"—she always uses that word when she's trying to be stern with us—"It will behoove you to get to work, or I'll call your Pa in here to give you a real licking."

Aunt Mavis, Lottie, and Anna stir up big batches of bread dough, plop it on the kitchen work table, and begin kneading it. Anna is sent to the spring house for butter, cream, and milk. When she returns to the kitchen, her arms wrapped around a big pan so full of chunks of yellow butter she can't see over the top of them, everyone begins laughing. "Anna's been in the sweet cream again," Aunt Mavis teases, and Anna, looking surprised at first, suddenly understands and quickly wipes off her mustache of foamy white cream with the back of her hand.

I don't stay around the kitchen any more than is necessary. But I do like it when Aunt Mavis tells stories about our family. I like to hear stories about Grandpa and Grandma long ago, when their families came by boat from Norway and then to North Dakota in covered wagons. Once I asked Aunt Mavis if she would teach me to talk Norwegian, and she said she didn't know how, except for a few words. "Grandma refused to speak Norwegian unless, of course, you couldn't speak English yet. And she wouldn't speak it to her kids and grandkids at all. 'We came to America because we wanted to get away from Norway,' I remember her sayin'. 'We've come unto a good land, and we're now Americans and we'll speak American. We're not Norwegians any more.'"

Aunt Mavis sits me down to pick stems off a million gooseberries heaped in big bowl. "Now, your Grandpa wasn't born in Norway. He was born along the way. Ja, he was born before they got to North Dakota. His parents were from Trondhjeim, so he always considered himself a Tronder." Now I understand what it means when the grown-ups talk about themselves as "Helgelanders" or "Telemarkings"—these were the places they came from in the old country.

"Your Grandpa's parents were travelin' by covered wagon and he was born in Wisconsin. And then they settled in Iowa for a year. We've still got family there, though I've never seen them. They were blacksmiths and hardware people, all of Grandpa's family. I've still got some of your grandfather's old hardware catalogs somewhere in the attic."

I like the part of the story where they were on the boat. I think Aunt Mavis does too, because it's so easy to get her to tell it. "It was a long hard trip to America from Norway—twelve weeks it was—and everyone had to bring with them whatever they would need on the boat—all their own food. They brought bricks of primost, a kind of cheese, and a bread they called flatbrod. Flatbrod was made round and had a hole in the middle so it could be stacked on a stick and kept dry from moldin'." As Aunt Mavis talks she moves back and forth, scrubbing potatoes in the sink and then putting them into the steaming, bubbling kettle on the stove. "They brought dried fish—Grandma used to laugh when she told the story, sayin' that they left Norway because they were all tired of eatin' dried fish.

"And they brought everything they needed to get started in their new homeland. Grandma carried her soft, homemade soap all the way from Norway in a little wooden box she used all her life here in America. Here it is still." Aunt Mavis went to the cupboard and brought out a wooden box. On the top was a picture of flowers and leaves made of all different kinds of wood worked to a nicety, worn smooth from Grandma's hands touching it every day for years and years. "Grandma brought this all the way from Norway." Aunt Mavis touched the box to her cheek and breathed in the smell of the old wood and, lifting her apron, dabbed at the corner of her eye. "She was so special in my life. She was funny and she was happy. I remember the gladness that shined in her eyes. She used to say to your ma and me, 'You can do anythin' you want to.' When we'd ask her to show us how to do somethin', she'd say, 'No, you're goin' to have to learn yourselves.' That was your grandma. She made the coverlet on your bed, and your Ma and Pa's steeplechase quilt too.

"Grandpa's father brought his tools with him, his blacksmith's tools— your Pa's still usin' them out in the barn. And he brought lasts to make wooden shoes, a set for each member of the family. Back in Norway the father made all the shoes for his family, and he still did it when he came to America."

Aunt Mavis sits down next to me again and helps with the gooseberries. I've been so busy listening to her story that I haven't got much done. "Well, it's a long story. But when Grandma was just a girl but old enough to go off on her own, she went down the Red River to Mapleton. She had her own shanty for the first year, made it herself out of blocks of sod cut from the prairie. Grandma worked as a bookkeeper in a hardware store. And what do you think? That was your Grandpa's hardware store and that's where Grandma and Grandpa met. They got married and Grandpa built them a beautiful two-story house. Grandma was so proud because it was the first house anywhere around with wood sidin'—by then, it was thought to be old fashioned to live in a sod or log house. That's this house, Peter. You're in your grandmother's kitchen. When I was your age I worked in this very kitchen, and not much has changed either."

Aunt Mavis dusts the tabletop with flour and begins kneading the lumps of dough into round loaves of dark rye bread. "Grandma planted those box elders in your front yard, just little whips they were then, and buffalo berries. My, she made wonderful berry pies. I remember sittin' at this very table with her while she was makin' buffalo berry pie. And she told me the story of the day, when she was a young girl, how she heard of the death of President Abraham Lincoln. Her father brought home a newspaper and read to her and her mother the story of Mr. Lincoln bein' shot. She remembered seein' a picture of the President—first time she ever saw his face—and thinkin' how kind and tired he looked. She remembered a great sadness comin' over the house, and that her mother cried. She told me how her father then asked her to take the newspaper to their closest neighbors—that would be the Skarstads—and then that paper would be passed from one place to another until everyone had read it."

While the bread's rising in the loaf, Anna fetches shiny glass jars of canned fruits and vegetables from the pantry. Stacked around the kitchen are crocks of pickled cucumbers, beets, beans, and apples. The smells of roast pork, boiled potatoes, cinnamon, cloves, and coffee all together make me mighty hungry. *Scratchscratchscratch,* Lottie shreds cabbage for a mountain of sauerkraut.

"Peter, we need some more stove wood." It seems like every minute Ma pulls open the big oven door and slides out a pan of hot rolls, or cookies, or buns, or biscuits. And in go loaves of bread rounded full over the tops of the pans. These days the cook stove never cools down and the kitchen is hotter than the platform up next to the engine's firebox.

A blackened kettle boils and steams full of parsnips. Another, its lid rattling away, is ready for the dozens of ears of corn Margit and Lottie have been shucking. It's fun having all our neighbors in the kitchen. Anna climbs up on the chair at one end of the long table. "Are your hands clean, Anna?" Ma always asks. Anna nods and then begins pulling little handfuls off of the soft mountain of bread dough. The sponge has set overnight on the stove and still feels warm. She kneads and plumps each handful of dough into a "pig" and lays it in a shallow pan, placing it just so in a row so as to fit in as many as she can. Aunt Mavis puts a molasses cookie down in front of Anna and winks a wink that says "Shhh, your Ma doesn't have to know." And then, with the same mischievous twinkle in her eyes, she gives me one too.

This morning, each morning while the thrashin' crew is here, Anna will make two hundred rolls. Some days Ma will have the bread pans laid out and Anna and Margit and Lottie will knead the dough into loaves. So many things to do, so many things to make and to cook, all those dishes to wash, and coffee, coffee, coffee! Anna and Margit's little girl, Bennie, begin hulling what seem like millions and millions of peas. They sit outside on the back porch with big bowls in their laps. Anna's gotten good at prying open the long, green pods and running her thumb down the inside, popping the peas into the bowl. The pile of peas always grows so much slower than the pile of hulls around their ankles on the porch.

Around ten o'clock Ma and Anna load the wagon with a huge laundry basket full of donuts and lefse—a very thin Norwegian potato pancake spread with butter and sprinkled with cinnamon and then rolled up—all wrapped and folded in a white cloth. Then they load on another basket full of cups and plates and wedge in, where they won't spill, blue-and-white speckled pots of coffee. Ma helps Anna climb up on the seat. "Now, Peter, go with Anna but this time let her drive the horses." She puts the reins in Anna's little hands and off we ride, out toward the big clouds of smoke and chaff and the thrashin' rig way off and little in the distance like a toy. It feels good to be getting out of the kitchen and back to the thrashin'.

The men come over by ones and twos for their lunch, and Anna climbs up on the engine with me and Mr. Parker. She likes it up here. I remember Anna saying once how she liked the feel of the engine, rocking back and forth in time to the steam cylinder, that it was like being on the back of a big, gentle ox. Mr. Parker told us that the old-timers still call the engine a "bull" traction engine, because in their day the engines were hauled from place to place by teams of oxen. When the men have eaten their lunch and the basket is empty to the last crumbs, Pa calls Anna to the wagon and sends her back to the house. She's happy that for the first time she can drive the team a ways by herself.

Today, at dinner, I decide to ask Pa if there might be a place for me on the thrashin' crew. He looks me up and down, and I stand as straight and tall as I can. Then he takes a moment to think it over. "You're a little fellow yet for the bundle wagons. Those big Belgians pull hard, and they'll get away 'less they feel two good strong hands on the reins. But now I s'pose you could drive the water wagon. Ya, sure, I'll bet you'd make a good tankee, Peter. Let's go ask Mr. Parker." Of course Pa and I know just where to find him, his hand on the throttle, humming a tune in time to his engine. Mr. Parker thinks about it too, all the time giving me a good looking over. He allows that he's short a couple of hands. Then he looks at me again, only this time with a little smile. "You've got yourself a job, young man." By jippers! I get to bring water to the engine.

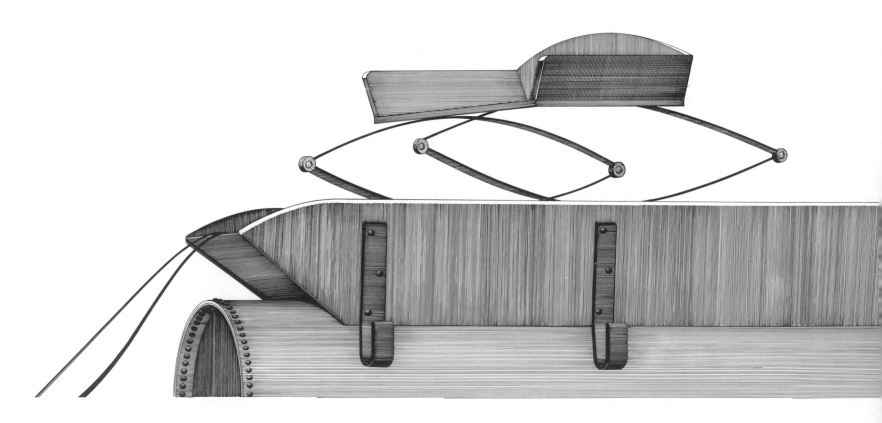

Pretty soon the men start calling me "tankee" and then I really feel like part of the crew. I wish Percy were here to see me. Most of the crew think the tankee's got an easy job. They think all he has to do is sit up on the seat and drive the team back and forth between the engine and the windmill pump. But he's a job to do, you betcha. He has to pump the water up into the tender, haul it back and then pump it into the water tank on the back of the engine. Mr. Parker says he needs seventy barrels and more a day. And the tankee's got to be right there when he's needed. If the engine runs too low on water the engineer would have to shut it down, right away, or else it could blow up.

That happened to Mr. Parker once—nearly running out of water, I mean, not blowing up. He told me the story about the time he was thrashin' Tosten Knutson's place one day last year. They had been thrashin' for quite a stretch when it dawned on him the tankee had been gone a long while. He kept looking at the water glass and searching the horizon. No tender in sight. So he grabbed the whistle cord and blew a long and three shorts, calling the tankee wherever he is to come back and fast.

Mr. Parker explained it all to me. You see, the top of the firebox—called the crown sheet—is the hottest part of the boiler, and so it has to stay covered with water. "No two ways 'bout it," as Mr. Parker would say. Now if the water level ever gets down far enough to where there's no water on the crown sheet—KERBANG!—the boiler will explode. It's sort of like what would happen if you left a kettle of water on the stove too long. As long as there's water, the bottom of the kettle is fine. But if the kettle boils dry, well, the bottom will crack or even melt.

Well time was running out. Mr. Parker could tell from the water glass that the water level was getting frightfully low. So he blew a long and three shorts again and still no tender in sight. "Goldang it!" I can just see him stomping back and forth getting madder and madder, and I can just hear him. "Where's that dadblasted water monkey gone to?" Turned out the windmill pump had stopped, not even a breeze, and the tankee had to go farther, way out to the pond at Kyvigs' place to get water. The tankee was still miles away when the water level was getting low enough as to make Mr. Parker awfully jittery.

Well, Mr. Parker did what he had to do. He blew one short—stop pitching—throttled down the engine to a stop and right then closed the dampers tight, yanked open the firebox door and threw ashes in on the fire. Saved the engine and probably the lives of the crew, he did, with his quick thinking. So the crew waited—not that they minded the rest. By and by, the tender and horses, galloping just as fast as they could and trailing a cloud of dust, hove into sight. Finally there was water to cool a thirsty engine and a riproarin' angry engineer.

It sure feels good to be working. Up till now I've just been sort of a kid around here. Of course kids work hard at thrashin' time. We carry water to the thrashers—we always put a little vinegar in the drinking water like Ma showed us, to make it a bit more pungent and better ease the thirst. We work in the kitchen, carrying in firewood and taking food out to the crews. Now, that's hard work, you betcha. There's breakfast and then morning lunch. Then there's dinner at about eleven o'clock. That's the big meal and a lot of food to carry. Then there's afternoon lunch at about three o'clock and finally, at about dusk, supper. We help stack the shocks in the field, too—there's always lots for kids to do just before the thrashermen come. They're like guests, you know. And Ma wouldn't think of having all the neighbors over to a messy place. So there's the house and barn to sweep, and floors to scrub clean, and maybe a wagon bed or two to paint. I help plug the mouse holes in the grain bin and sew patches on any grain sacks that are torn. Anna gets to polish the tack and spend time where she'd rather be, in with the horses. And we make lots of trips into Fargo to buy supplies.

Of course we always have time for fun. We kids always see to that. We get way up in the straw stack and tumble down to the ground. We play thrashers, pitching straw into a make-believe separator and handling the throttle of our make-believe engine. Sometimes I'd throw straw and chaff way up in the air pretending I was the wind stacker. Aunt Mavis told us once that when she was a girl and the grownups were all out busy thrashin', she'd sneak into the big barn. There was a rope hanging high up between the two haylofts—it's still there—and she'd swing on it from one loft, all the way across the barn, let go and fly into the hay piled on the other side. Then she got a look on her face like someone who's let a secret out. "Oh Peter, I wouldn't want your Ma and Pa to know I told you 'bout that. Might give you some wrong ideas." Then she winked and hurried back to the kitchen. She needn't worry none. Anna and I agreed it sounded too scary anyway. Then again, maybe tomorrow, while everyone's eating supper . . .

———

Something happened today, something scary. I was standing next to Mr. Haugen waiting my turn to wash up for dinner. And I look over at one of his hands. Well, where two middle fingers should have been on his left hand there are just these two little stubs. And then, as he rolls up his sleeve, I can see a long, deep, ugly brown scar all the way up his arm. The arm seems caved in, and the hand doesn't seem to work as well as a hand ought to. I try to feel the hurt of that happening, wonder if he cried, wonder if I could've stood it. I can't take my eyes off that arm, and I begin to feel all sweaty, and shaky and like I'm going to be sick. The next thing I know I'm running—I don't know where, just anywhere—away from that terrible scar.

Well, for the rest of the day I've been looking at hands and arms. Just hands and arms. It seems as if that's all I can see. I don't see bundle pitchers and drivers and separator men anymore, just hands with missing fingers. It seems everyone has lost a finger or part of one—well, a few of the men have anyway.

Later, when we stop for afternoon lunch, I get up my courage, go up to Mr. Haugen and ask him how it happened, the arm and the fingers. Mr. Haugen touches his sleeve and then pulls his arm close in against his body, like he's protecting it, trying to keep me from looking at it. He has a hurt look in his eyes, like he wants to run, and I wish I hadn't asked. But then his face softens and he seems more all right again.

"Well, Peter," he says, "Up till now I've not thought much about that terrible day, just put it out of my mind, you know. But maybe there's a lesson in it for a young shaver like you. And maybe it's time for this old-timer to own up to it." Mr. Haugen eases down into a pile of straw and pulls from his shirt pocket a small white cloth bag of Bull Durham tobacco. With his good hand he holds a piece of cigarette paper between his thumb and middle finger, presses down with his forefinger to make a trough and pours into it a line of brown tobacco. Then he closes the bag by pulling the string tight in his teeth, slips it back into his pocket, runs the edge of the paper along the tip of his tongue and rolls a cigarette. He taps it into the palm of his hand a couple of times, strikes a wooden match with his thumbnail—*snap*—lights his cigarette, takes a puff and squints far out into the distance, the way folks do when they have weighty matters to discuss.

"I was about your age when it happened, not much older." And Mr. Haugen tells me how he had reached in too close to a belt on the separator, and how his hand and arm had been pulled into the machine. The engineer saw the commotion, heard his screams all the way back at the engine and stopped that instant, but, of course, it was too late. "I remember my Pa rippin' off his shirt and wrappin' my arm, carryin' me and layin' me in the wagon and then jumpin' up on the seat and drivin' the horses hard, as fast as they could go to town, to Dr. Boekmann's. My sister Emma had jumped in the wagon just before our father drove off and held me. We had to go all the way to Fargo, twenty miles and a long, dusty, painful, joltin' ride it was in that old wooden wagon—seemed like it took forever. Sure it felt that way for my Pa and Emma too. Well, old Dr. Boekmann saved my arm, all right, but there wasn't much he could do for the fingers, all mashed like they were.

"I was lucky, Peter. A lot of good men have been killed by these machines. Now don't get me wrong. I'm not against progress and all that. But it sure seems like farmin' wasn't so dangerous before these contraptions came along." Mr. Haugen holds his arm out to the sun in front of us, looks at it like an old friend he's found again. All this time he's turning his rough, horny hand this way and that, spreading his fingers and then making a fist over and over. "I've done a life's work with this stiff old arm, a thumb and only two fingers. Ya, sure, a life's work." Two short barks of the whistle call us back to thrashin' again. All around us, the men groan as they get up, slapping the straw from their grease-stiffened overalls and limp slowly, stiffly back to the separator and the waiting wagons.

That's not all of it. Something's kept me away from the engine and the separator today. Mr. Parker must be thinking it funny that I haven't been around the rig at all this afternoon—usually, I can't wait, and stand around hoping he'll ask me to do some work around the engine. I don't know, it's just that now the belts and spinning gears and pulleys have a different look—mean, hurtful, and scary.

———

Aunt Mavis and I took the wagon into Fargo to buy some roasts, butter, and cheese for the thrashers. Ma and Anna usually churn all our butter, but there's just not enough for this big crew. I like to go along 'cause Mr. Beebe at the creamery always gives me a glass of cold buttermilk. And whenever we go to the butcher he always gives us kids a free wiener. Today we'll stop at the ice house to get two blocks of ice so we can make real ice cream with berries on top for the thrashers. The ice is covered with sawdust, which is what it's been stored in since last winter when it was cut from a frozen lake over in Minnesota. When we get it home we'll put it in the barn and cover it all up with straw so it'll keep a few more weeks that way. But before turning the team around and heading back home, we've got one thing more to do that Aunt Mavis and I enjoy most when we come to town: stopping at the railroad station. Today we're to pick up an engine part that's coming by train all the way from Racine, Wisconsin.

Aunt Mavis loves to watch trains and it's about time for the 1:15 from Minneapolis. While we're waiting on the bench on the station platform she tells me the story of once when she was about five or six, she was standing just about where we are now, eating some cookies— they were cinnamon-walnut cookies (Aunt Mavis always remembers little facts like that). Well, the conductor came up to her and asked if she'd sell him one of her cookies. She thought that was fine, and told him she had bought the cookies for five cents each. He gave her a dime. She didn't have any change, but he smiled, thanked her and said it didn't matter. And that seemed to be that.

"It bothered me, though," she said, "and the next day I went back with another cookie for the conductor. Well, I waited and waited, and when he didn't appear I just climbed up the steps of a coach, climbed up into a seat and waited for him. It was a while, and he didn't come, but all of a sudden there was a loud whistle from the engine, a conductor called 'aaaall aboard,' the train lurched, the engine began puffin' slowly at first and then faster and faster and I was on my way—but to where?

"Well, let me tell you I was scared. I just began a-bawlin' and the conductor, and the train master and porters came runnin' from both ends of the train. It took them awhile, but they got me into a seat and quieted me down. They put me off at the next station and telegraphed back to Fargo that I'd be on the late afternoon train. The station master kept me with him all that time, gave me milk and cookies (oatmeal raisin, as I recall) and taught me my name in Morse code—still remember it." Aunt Mavis taps out her name just like a telegraph key on the kitchen table. "I wasn't cryin' anymore, but all the time I was thinkin' of the lickin' I would get when I got home. Well, it was dark when I did finally step down once again onto the platform in Fargo. My mother and father were there waitin' with the horses and wagon, very happy to see me. And they even brought me a cookie—a cinnamon-walnut cookie—to eat all by myself on the way home."

3

Mountains of Wheat

THIS MORNING there are millions of bright stars overhead in a black sky. I'm warm in my bedroll but my face and ears sting with cold. The frost on the barn roof glows all silvery in the starlight. All around me are snoring, wheezing thrashers, fallen exhausted into a deep, tired sleep. A cowbell clunks in the distance. Somewhere a dog wuffles. The bedroll next to me stirs, coughs, lays quiet again. *Owowowooooo* a coyote howl sends a shiver up and down my body. I hear footsteps in the frosted stubble and, rolling over and raising up on my elbow, I can see a lantern winking in the barnyard. Mr. Parker's headed this way, past the barn, through the gate, and out toward the black hulk of the engine, the separator and hay racks silhouetted against the starry sky. The little light swings and bounces across the dark field and then I see it rise up and rest on top of the engine. I hear the clank of the latch, the groan of the firebox door hinges, and the ringing of the iron poker stirring the coals into flames. Time to go to work. I untangle myself from my bedroll and, all awake in the frosty air, run out to the engine.

"Is that you, Peter?" Mr. Parker peers into the dark, until I walk into the lantern's circle of light. "I thought so. No one but a thrasher would

be up and around this time of night. Well, now that you're here you can give me a hand." He smiles. "I s'pose that's why you're here." Mr. Parker opens the smokebox door and holds the lantern up to see inside. I can see a lot of holes—the ends of the tubes that carry smoke and heat from the firebox, through the water in the boiler, and then into the smokebox and up the stack. "Soot collects in the tubes," Mr. Parker says, "and that cuts down on the heat that can get to the water and make steam. A good engineer will clean his flues every day," Mr. Parker says, like he's reciting in front of his class at school. He picks up a long iron rod with a flue scraper on the end and pushes it through each tube

all the way to the firebox end. He cleans out some of the flues and then hands me the flue scraper. "Here you go, Peter, finish up the last of 'em on the bottom. And when you're done with that I'll give you your first lesson in firin' an engine."

All during thrashin' time the fire in the engine never goes out. At night the engineer banks the fire—covers it with ashes—so that there're always hot coals in the morning to start another fire. Engines burn all kinds of fuel—coal, oil, straw, even corn cobs. We're burning wood, a whole pile of cord wood stacked there on the wagon. The first thing Mr. Parker shows me is how to shake out the ashes, pile wood in the firebox, and then stir the fire—"Careful, now, you don't want to dump all the hot coals." He shows me how to make a small fire at first, so that all the iron plates and rivets heat up slowly, evenly. "Keep your eye on the steam gauge and let me know when it shows ten pounds of steam."

While I'm getting a good fire going, Mr. Parker's climbing all over the engine with his oil can and a rag. He makes sure all the grease cups are full and that there's plenty of cylinder oil. "A good engineer who takes pride in his work will keep his machines lookin' clean and polished," he says, reaching over the boiler, wiping away the runs and drips to keep everything bright. "But do ya know the real reason a good engineer wipes down his engine all the time?" I shake my head. "Because if you're always rubbin' over the engine parts, touchin' everythin', you can feel, feel in your hands, the first signs of trouble—a loose nut, a vibration that's not s'posed to be there, a hot, dry bearin'." Mr. Parker's tugging on things, feeling for looseness. "You listen, too, learn the sounds of your engine when it's runnin' well. Remember them. Then, if you do hear a clunk, or squeak, or rattle that's not s'posed to be there, you'll know somethin's not right and fix it before it breaks down."

"The gauge shows ten pounds of steam now," I call out. Mr. Parker jumps up beside me on the platform, rests his oil can on a little shelf and opens a valve that sends steam *hissssing* up through the stack. "The steam goin' up the stack causes a draft," he shouts over the noise. "Now look into the firebox—but don't leave it open too long." Sure enough the fire leaps red and hot off the coals. "I think it could use a stick or two more wood, Mr. Parker."

"You're a good learner, Peter. Go ahead, fireman, throw in a couple. Remember how I showed you?" Faster now, the pointer of the steam gauge moves up toward twenty pounds, twenty-five, thirty pounds, thirty-five . . . "Forty pounds, Mr. Parker."

"Good job of firin', Peter, she's ready to run."

Just then Pa arrives a bit surprised to see me up and working already, covered head to boots with soot and grease. He and the separator man, Mr. Booras, walk all around the machine squirting oil into bearings and spreading grease onto sprockets and gears. They tug on belts to make sure they're tight, stopping now and then to adjust a slack belt. Then Mr. Booras grabs up a handful of chaff and throws it into the air, watching it drift off. He's seeing where the wind's coming from, to make sure the bundle pitchers won't be pitching into the wind with all the chaff and straw blowing back into their faces. Sometimes the prairie wind's so strong, it'll blow the drive belt right off the pulleys, if the engine and separator aren't set up right. Meanwhile, Pa picks up a few heads of wheat and pinches them between his fingers. He can tell by the way the grain heads crumble if the wheat's dry enough to thrash. "Looks good, Bill. Wasn't much dew last night, so I think we'll be ready for an early start."

By now you can just see a thin line of blue on the horizon, the first light of dawn, but it's still frosty. A few of the crew are gathering around the engine and separator. Some hunch over steaming cups of coffee clutched between their hands, breathing in the warmth. A few still have their bedrolls over their shoulders like shawls. Others stand alongside the engine's firebox, rubbing their hands together. "Peter, check the water and fill up the tank. We'll soon be startin' up."

Toooot! Toooot! Two long whistle blasts break the morning stillness—and send a shiver up my back—to signal the crew that a new thrashin' day is about to begin. Mr. Parker opens the throttle and a great puff of smoke shoots up into the blue-black sky. *Tucka-tucka-tucka-tucka* the steam engine comes to life. *Slip-slap-slip-slap-slip-slap* the belt weaves up and down like a thing alive bringing from the separator a rattling of gears. "Yaahoooo!" Mr. Parker lets out a whoop and waves his hat. "We're the first ones a-goin' this mornin'." All the engineers hereabouts try to be the first to start the day, and Mr. Parker is proud to be running before any other whistles are heard out on the land. "Let me tell you, Peter," Mr. Parker says, shaking his finger at me like my teacher does when she scolds, "any engineer who hasn't got steam up and can't blow his whistle an hour before sunrise is a lazy good-fer-nothin'. You betcha. Shouldn't even be allowed to call himself an engineer, I say." Soon, here and there, the whistles of other thrashin' outfits sound in the distance, one by one starting their day. "Let 'er fly, boys. We're goin' to thrash a mountain of wheat today."

Everyone gets to working. High up on the grain stacks the spike pitchers, standing up to their suspender ends in wheat, begin flinging bundles with big, bold sweeps of their arms. The sky's getting brighter with each minute and the rising sun flashes off the fork tines like sparks.

Swing back, jab into a bundle, lift and swing out, shaking the bundle off—always grain heads first—onto the moving feeder. Swing back, jab, lift and swing out, swing back, jab, lift and swing out, swing back, jab, lift and swing out—the pitchers fall into an easy rhythm. But it's hard work. Already shirts darken and faces shine and run with sweat.

Riddle-raddle-riddle-raddle-riddle-raddle, chains and sprockets and pulleys and gears power the thrashin' machinery hidden inside the separator. Cutter bars flash out, cut the bands and pull the grain in like steel claws. Pa says if you could look inside the separator now you'd see the wheat being beaten between the whirring teeth of the cylinder and concaves. Then it travels along racks that shake the grain out of the straw. A powerful fan lifts the straw and chaff from the grain and blows it out the wind stacker in a great roostertail, thirty or forty feet into the air. You can see it for miles across the flat prairie. Under the wind stacker is growing a mountain of straw and chaff and dust. And the grain fills a waiting wagon.

There's more to pitching bundles than lots of hard work and getting itchy straw down your shirt. The bundles want to go into the feeder just right, not too many at once. Four bundle pitchers have to work hard to feed a hungry thrashin' machine, but you'd better not throw in too much at once. You can tell when a pitcher's slugged the machine, clogged the cylinder with too much straw. The engine slows and labors hard and Mr. Parker shoots one of those glances at you over the top of his spectacles. Pa says your ears'll tell you how well you're pitching. "Keep it hummin' at an even pitch—not too high, not too low, you want a middlin' hum."

Toot! Toot! Toot! Bundle wagon drivers hustle. The bundle pitchers are almost to the bottom of their stacks. Full racks teetering with wheat

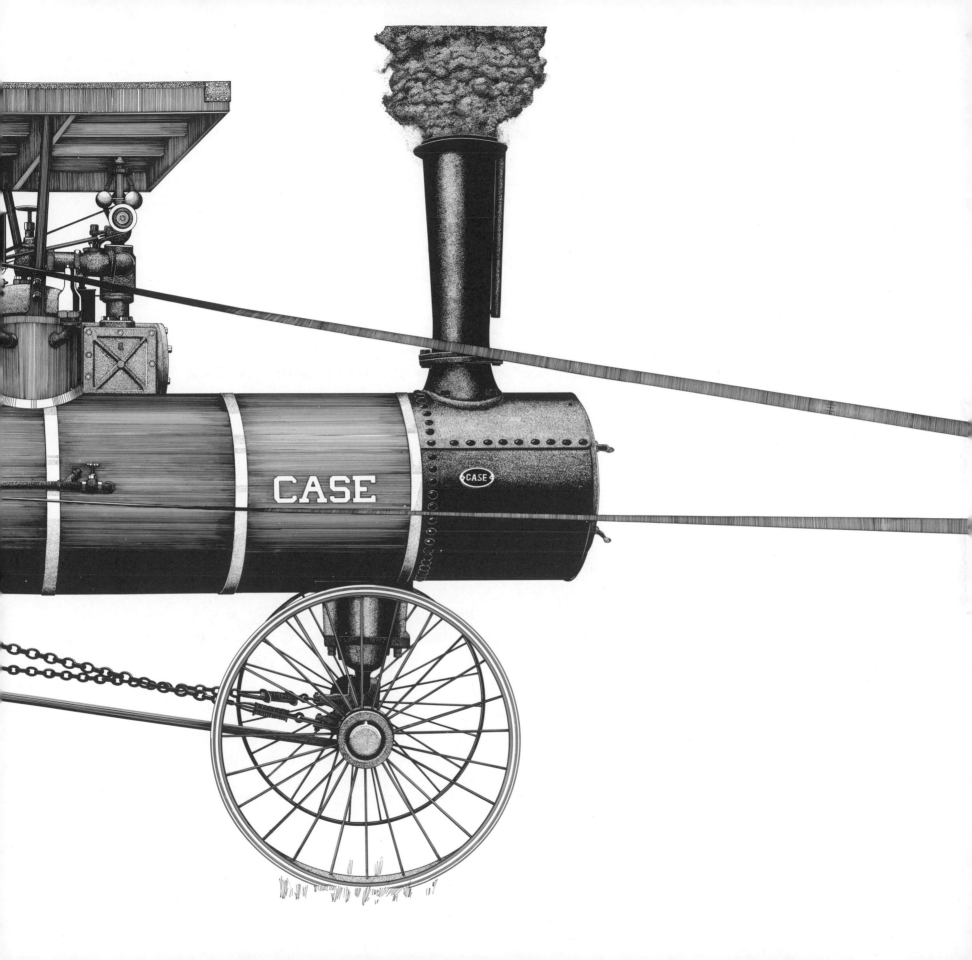

piled high are coming, pulled by teams of strong, brawny Belgians, traces jingling, their heads nodding against the bit and halters. "G'up there," "haw," "whoa," "back," "back," the drivers cluck to their prancing horses, "hah," "haw," "gee." Look at them, horses and drivers all locked together.

Uncle Arne says a good field pitcher takes pride in the way he loads the racks. "Pile up as big a load as you can ('cept, maybe, at the end of the day when sore muscles and dusk tell you that this has to be the last load). And be careful that the sheaths are stacked with the grain heads in toward the center of the wagon. Thrashin' really begins on the rack's jarrin', rattlin' ride across furrowed fields to the separator, you know. There'll be a heap of grain on that wagon floor by the time you git there."

Two full racks stand alongside the separator. The bundle pitchers are climbing high up onto the full racks and Mr. Parker signals with two sharp blasts of the whistle to start again. Meantime, the drivers head back out to the fields with their empty racks where the teams of field pitchers are waiting. The air is filled with working noises, the jostling and yelling to the teams, the soft breathing of the engine, belts slip-slapping, the separator whirring and clattering, and the stream of grain—*sssssssssssss*—filling the wagons. I touch Pa on the arm and point to little Anna atop the fuel bunker. She's fallen asleep with the gentle rocking of the steam engine. Pa puts aside his fork, takes Anna into his arms and lays her down in a soft pile of straw.

"Peter! You'd better put a little hustle in your knees there." Mr. Parker's call reminds me it's time for water. I pump the engine's tank full, but now the tender's empty, and so it's out to the windmill. "G'up horses, let's go get us another load of water."

The windmill's out in a corner of our section near a little clump of willows, box elders, and elms, all turning yellow now. There are old stumps there too, reminders of trees Grandpa felled with his axe and then dragged out behind oxen. He sawed the trees into timbers and planks for their house—our house—the barn, the springhouse, the little blacksmithing shed, and wagon boxes. From one of these trees, Aunt Mavis told us, he made the bed Ma and me and Anna were born in. These willows were big even way back in Grandpa's day. Willows are thirsty trees; they like to have their feet wet and they told Grandpa to dig a well here.

Grandpa and Grandma, my pa's parents, are buried here under the big elm, too; this is our family graveyard. I like to sit here, in the little clearing, with the stones, and with my grandparents. The branches of the old trees are twittering with the whistles and calls of the wrens, and titmice, and pewees—*pee-oo-wee, pee-oo*—and so many birds I don't know. Coming from the pond, on the other side of the wood, I can hear *whap, whap, whap*—beavers slapping mud on their dams with their broad tails. Pa's sister, Mollie, is here too. He doesn't talk much about her except to say, with sadness in his eyes, that she was taken from us by smallpox.

The name on Grandpa and Grandma's stones is different from ours—Fjelstad, Laverans and Kjersti Fjelstad. When I first saw these stones I was just a little kid. I can remember standing in front of what seemed like a big stone then, tracing the cut letters with my finger and then asking Pa who these people were. "They're my parents, Peter," he said, "your grandparents."

Then why is their name different from ours? Pa said Fjelstad was the name Grandma and Grandpa brought with them from the old country. And it happened when he went to school the first day. The teacher changed his name and the names of the other Norwegian children. "She gave us the name 'Fisk.' Papa was unhappy about giving up his name. You betcha, he was angry and refused to do it, at first. But the teacher told him that we had to change our names to become Americans, and well, it was your Grandma who got him to do it. So your Ma and me have American-soundin' names. And you do too. In the old country you'd be Peder, Peder Fjelstad. Some of the old folks here 'bouts keep their old names still."

Pa told me once that Grandpa rode on the very first Great Northern train to come into Fargo, from Chicago I think. Grandpa settled here and planted his acres to wheat. He didn't have a reaper or thrashin' machine—too newfangled, Pa says, for old-world Lutherans. Pa says he can still see Grandpa out in the field cradling his wheat, cutting it with broad strokes of his scythe, his strong arms swinging back and forth, back and forth, leaving a swath of fallen stalks behind him. He can see Grandpa resting every so often to wipe the sweat from his face and to push his suspenders back up onto his shoulders. Now and then Grandpa stopped, pulled a whetstone from his pocket, spat on it and then ran it slither-slather along the keen edge of the long, curved blade—*smira, smira, smira*. Later, Grandma and Grandpa and Pa—well he wasn't Pa then—would beat the grains off the straw by hand with a flail. Pa says Grandpa worked from sunup to sundown but, even so, he could cradle two, maybe three acres in a day, at the very most. I wonder sometimes what . . .

Toooooooot! Toooooooot! Toooooooot! The engine! Water! Oh-oh! Here I sit dreaming and Mr. Parker's needing water. So long Grandma and Grandpa, this tankee's got work to do.

———

A long, steady whistle calls to the bundle pitchers to stop, calls in the drivers and teams, calls the men to come eat and rest. Dinner time. The steam engine slides to a stop, stilling the belt and the separator's whine. All around are grunts of thirst and empty bellies and heat and sore muscles. The bundle pitchers plant their forks in the wheat with a jab, loosen bandannas from around their necks to mop their sweaty faces dusted with chaff and wipe around the sweat bands inside their hats. The noonday sun sets the fields shimmering and dazzles my eyes. There's no shadows out here now except the deep darkness under the engine and separator. It's quiet. From high above comes a chorus of honking. We hold our hands up against the sun and look up to see a flock of black and gray Canada geese winging their way across the sky in long, shifting Vs. The air is still but here and there a puff of breeze brings the manure pile to our noses and lifts a swirl of dust and chaff into the air. Cloud shadows move across the stubbly fields.

A line forms at the water bucket, each man taking his turn to dip the dented ladle and sip cool water and the bitterness of the old metal through parched lips. Another line forms at the washbasins where Anna has set out towels and big brown bars of homemade soap. She stands timid, peering from behind a wagon, watching the men splashing water into their faces, letting the coolness stream down their forearms. She's wondering at the tall black man waiting in line, talking in soft sounds, not at all like the voices our ears are so used to.

With their hands and sunburned faces scrubbed clean, the thrashers make their way to the wagon where Ma and Aunt Mavis have put out all the fixings for dinner. Jugs of milk and pitchers of iced tea. Pot roasts carved into juicy slices, bread cut thick from the loaf, Anna's rolls and mounds of butter scooped right from the churn this morning. There're big bowls of cole slaw, and potato salad, and pickles and plates stacked with steaming ears of corn. For dessert there's Lottie Hanson's molasses cake, four gooseberry pies and big pots of hot coffee. As the men file by nodding thanks and heaping their plates, the food just disappears, "like dew in the midsummer sun," as Ma always says. She pours steaming cups of coffee and stands close by drying her hands in her apron, proud from all the good things being said about her cooking.

I get to sit with the thrashers this year, by jiminy. Over sounds of eating, the clinking of knives and forks on plates, munching corn off the cob, slurping of coffee and milk, there's talk of the crop and the market, and times past, good and bad. "This looks like it's goin' to be a good harvest," Mr. Parker says, reaching his knife across the table for a dab of butter, "maybe the best we've had fer some time now." Yep, that's true, but all agree with nodding heads that there's no reason to take too much comfort in it. Every farmer around these tables has known years when they plowed and seeded as they always had, worked hard and done their best, only to see their crops destroyed by hail storms, drought, insects, the black stem rust, or flood. "Who will ever forget, back there in aught-six when it rained for fifty-three days and just flooded out the fields?" Mr. Solheim recalls the worst year in memory— back before my time—when the weather was dry and the grasshoppers took the whole crop. Farmers set fire to part of their wheat hoping to burn the grasshoppers too. Some of the older men nod, their eyes hard with memories of how they suffered so that season. There's mention of neighbors who've lost their farms and had to move on somewhere, and it all of a sudden gets quiet like we're at prayer. "Yup, it's root-hog-or-die for the farmer most any year," says one of the field hands. "Ya, sure," Pa says, "we're all hopin' for a good year, hopin' that we'll have a full granary, enough to get us through to next year, and maybe have enough money left over even to pay some to the bank." The hired hands talk of their hopes, of putting aside enough money to buy the farm they've dreamed of, or to marry their girl back home, maybe to start a new life somewhere, buy a place or a thrashin' outfit of their own.

And I start to thinking about old Percy, how he worked so hard every year, so many years. Dinner around these tables was his favorite time, a time to tell his stories. What had he worked for? He never talked of wants or dreams. As clear as day, I can see him sitting at the thrashers' table—right over there—nibbling sausage off the point of his knife, his eyes smiling, telling about life on the road. I miss him and I'm a little angry with him, too, for not coming back this year. But surely he'd come if he could. Maybe next year, or in the spring, with the plowing teams.

~ 4 ~
Movin' On

I T's LATE and we're all bedded down in the barn and up in the haymow. Here and there a few men sit in the flickering light of kerosene lanterns playing pinochle or just talking, telling stories—tall tales, most likely. Outside it's cold. The first hint of winter is on the wind, and the thrashers talk of a hard freeze tonight. It gets quieter as one by one the lanterns blink out and the men curl up in their bedrolls. The barn is still now except for the horses in their stalls stomping and snorting every so often. I'm just at the edge of sleep and somewhere in the night the *hooooot, hooot* of an owl . . .

"Peter, is that you?" It's Pa crouching down beside me, shaking my arm. "Time to get up son," he whispers hoarsely. I roll back my cozy, warm bedroll, and the cold nips my ears and nose. "I just come to tell you you won't be drivin' the water wagon today." I sit up, my mind going, trying to figure out why, what's wrong. Oh-oh, that's it, yesterday, getting back late with the water. Mr. Parker's told Pa about it. "It's all right, son," Pa touches my shoulder. "It's just that one of the grain wagon drivers is sick and has to go home. You've been handlin' your two-horse team so well, I reckon you're strong enough to handle a four-

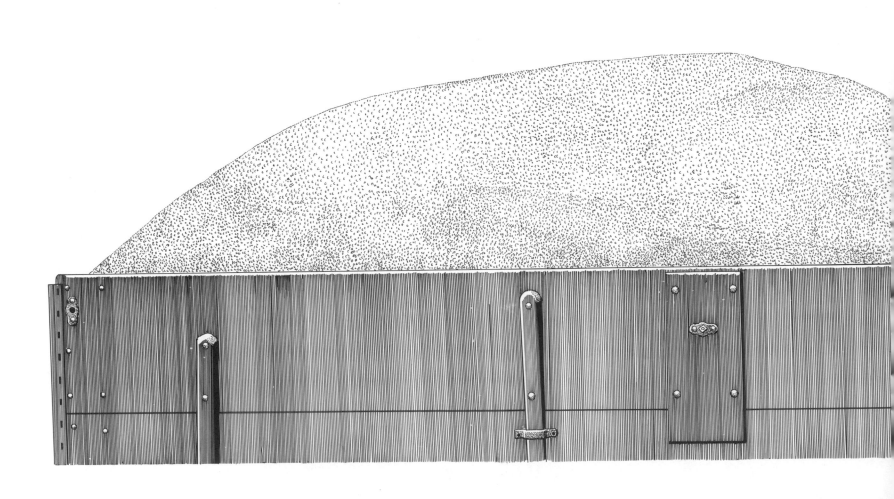

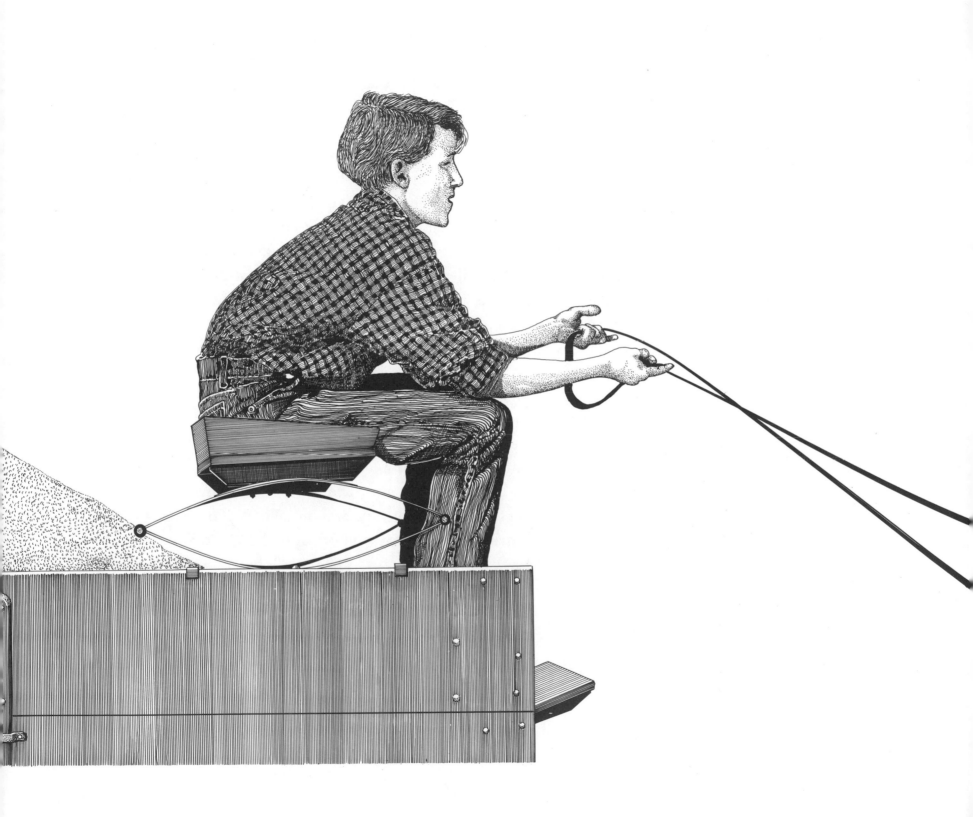

horse team. Besides, I'll be driving one of the other wagons and we'll be together. What d'ya say, Peter, want to give it a try?" My own four-horse team! And I get to take the wagon all the way into town and back. "Sure Pa, you betcha."

Pa and me, we work together. He takes the harness down off the pegs in the barn, lays it on my shoulders and arms so it all stays untangled. Then we lay it up on the horses, careful to get everything buckled and cinched down right. When we have all four horses harnessed, we lead them outside and hitch them up to the old green wagon, my wagon today. "Your grandpa built this wagon, Peter. I was just a young pup, but I can still remember him workin' over there on the forge, hammerin', sparks flyin' all around us, makin' all the hardware and the iron tires." Pa goes over to one of the bright yellow wheels and touches the shiny, rough steel. "That's what I remember best, him makin' those tires. Of course, we've had to make two new wheels for busted spokes, and your grandpa's tires wore out years ago—I made these myself just the way he showed me how. But it's his wagon still, and you'll be up there on the seat today."

Pa climbs up beside me and helps me get the team over alongside the separator and under the wagon spout. "The grain is measured out in the weigher there before it goes into the wagon. When your wagon's full—the separator man will tell you—pull off over there and wait for me. Good time to water your horses. Then we'll head out to the elevator."

Handling the four horses is hard work. Sometimes I have to dig my heels into the footboard and pull my whole body back against the reins to slow them. I can't imagine what it must be like to drive six horses, or eight! I remember watching Mr. Torgrimson plow with eight horses—eight abreast—pulling a four-bottom plow up a rise just as easy as you please. You must have to be awfully strong to drive eight horses, though.

The road is busy with grain wagons from all around coming and going to the elevator. I can just see it now, in the distance, sticking up out of the prairie, the only thing for miles around. Pa says a couple trains will be coming through while we're in town. There are always flat cars loaded with shiny, new, brightly painted engines, reapers, separators, wagons, and plows.

Pa has business with the elevator man, so after we get the teams tied up, I wander along the tracks over to the station. It's quiet—just the wind, voices somewhere in the freight depot, and the click of the telegraph. It sounds like the wind's coming up but no, turns out to be a locomotive, chuffing away in the distance. Now I can see it, out toward the west, gray smoke billowing into the dusty blue sky, wavering in the heat, weaving along the tracks. The engineer whistles at the grade crossing down by the elevator. The puffing grows louder and louder until the Great Northern giant rumbles right by me, hissing steam, shaking the ground, and smelling of coal smoke and hot oil. The locomotive's bell clangs louder and louder. I wave and the engineer waves back a gloved hand and then reaches into the cab. Brakes screech, the freight cars shudder, slow, and then the whole train jolts to a stop.

The train's almost all boxcars for wheat, and it's so long the end disappears around a curve. The caboose must be way out on the prairie somewhere. Our wheat'll be in one of those cars—on its way, Pa told me, to the big flour mills in Minneapolis. Dozens of men lean on bedrolls, sit and stand on top of the brown wooden boxcars, the hoboes, tramps, and field workers Pa told me about. Men appear in the open boxcar doors, blinking in the sunlight. One, a boy really, wearing a cap, peers out, looks around and then jumps down. He's smaller than me. Our eyes meet for a second, but he's excited about something and begins yelling up at the men on the car and then to me and the people at the station. I can't hear what he's shouting but several of the men drop backwards down the ladders on the sides of their cars and gather in a knot around the door. There's trouble. I start heading over, not sure at first, and then start running toward the boxcar too.

"I can't wake him," I hear the boy cry. Two of the men climb up into the boxcar and disappear into the darkness. I can hear the boy just sobbing inside, all around me a murmur of voices. "What's happenin'?" "Who's in there?" The men who rode in on the car tops crowd around trying to find out who's in the boxcar and where he got on, and had anyone noticed him. "He got on at Spokane," someone says, "or maybe Whitefish, can't remember for sure." Someone else in the crowd says, "He was goin' to get off here in Fargo. That's why the boy tried to wake him up."

Suddenly the two men appear again in the bright light of the door, dragging something I can't see from back in the shadows. Someone reaches up and takes hold of the boy and sets him down. More men gather around, and all I can see is a man being handed out to the crowd, his arms dangling down loose, their arms raised up to take him—careful now, he's heavy—and lay him gently on the ground. In the moment he floats above the crowd I get only a quick look, but I can see that he's wrapped in an old, tattered bedroll and newspapers. He wears the same overalls we all wear, and a red bandanna around his neck. His face is all but hidden in a mop of matted gray hair and beard.

A couple men are down on the ground with him, one with his ear pressed to the old man's chest. "He's dead," the man who's been listening for a heartbeat says, solemn. Everybody hushes. A few take off their hats and press them to their chests. Some cross themselves. "Must've froze to death crossin' Montana last night," another says. "It was mighty cold and snowin' too, by the time we got to Williston."

There's something about that poor stranger . . . I have to see him, and I shove my way through the crowd. Please let me through, I have to . . . suddenly I'm standing not inches from the man on the ground. His skin is so pale, like ice. The backs of his hands, resting across his chest, are crisscrossed with blue veins. His eyes are open, cloudy blue, staring up into the sky. Then someone reaches over and brushes his eyes closed. I kneel down and touch the old gray bearded head cradled in the little boy's lap. He's crying, kind of rocking the old man back and forth in his arms, gasping for breath, scrubbing his eyes with the back of his hand like he wanted the sight to go away, like I did. "He's my friend," the boy sobs, "He's my friend, Percy."

Pa must have picked me up and carried me back to the wagon, because the next thing I know I'm sitting next to him, my head buried in his chest, his arms around me. The train is gone and the tracks are empty and quiet, and it's just as though nothing's happened. "He was on his way, wasn't he Pa? He hadn't really forgotten me and Anna, had he?"

"He was on his way, Peter, I'm sure of that. What a shame. He got so close, too. He almost made it, didn't he?"

"But why did it have to happen like that, Pa, him all alone in the cold night?"

"Percy's life was ridin' trains, son. I think this is the way he would have wanted it to be." We sit and talk for a long while, remembering Percy. Trains come and go. Pa allows that Percy had always done in his life what he wanted to do, that we shouldn't feel sorry for him in any way. "No, Peter, he wouldn't want sorry feelin's or pity, not Percy." Pa says how he'd always liked Percy since that day years ago when he first showed up at our place asking for a job. "I know he was your friend, and I'll miss him too, Peter. I've known many a field hand and thrasher in my time, but weren't none his like."

——

Friday morning. Anna, Ma, and Aunt Mavis have brought out breakfast—corn meal, porridge, sausages, fried potatoes, bread and butter, eggs, donuts, and, of course, the huge pots of coffee, sugar, and sweet cream. Mr. Parker got steam up early, blowing the whistle at about four-thirty. Ma said I didn't have to work today if I didn't feel up to it. But I feel better being busy. I've already made a run for water and back. It seems a whole day has gone by, that the bundle and grain wagons have been coming and going for hours now, but it's only six o'clock. The sun's barely up. I can tell winter's on its way from how low the sun is in the sky and how much later each morning it stays frosty.

I've felt all morning there was something strange about today, though I can't put my finger on it. There's excitement in the air, and Pa especially is talking and laughing with the men more than usual—still I feel sad.

"We've plenty of water to finish the job, Peter," Mr. Parker calls to me from the engine, "probably by mid-morning. Why don't you come on up here and be my fireman while we do these last wagon loads." Now I know what's happening. It's not just poor old Percy. The thrashin' will be over in an hour or two. The engine, the thrashin' crew, and the neighbors will all leave, move on to the next farm. They'll be gone till next fall, a whole year. Anna and me, we'll be back in school on Monday. Aunt Mavis will return to Fargo and the kitchen will be quiet again. Gee whillikers, these three days have gone by fast!

Mr. Parker and I are looking out over the engine, out along the belt to the separator to Pa and the other pitchers, working their way down to the very last of the bundles. I like these smells of hot, oily metal, of woodsmoke, chaff, and prairie dust. The roll and thrum of the engine traveling up through my feet and legs make me feel like I'm part of the machine. And I know this engine now. I can read the water glass and steam gauge. I know when it's time to turn on the injector and how much water the boiler needs. I know to check the try cocks to make sure the gauge is right, that there's really plenty of water above the crown sheet. After all, I've got to think of the safety of my crew.

Tuck . . . tuck tuck-a-tuck, tuck, tuck—Oh-oh, the engine is laboring, out of time. Must be the pitchers have slugged the separator. I'll just move the throttle a notch or two—*Tuck, tuck-a,* little more power—*tuck, tuck-a-tuck-a-tuck-a-tuck-a*—there, she's running smoothly again, sounding good. "You know, Mr. Parker, this throttle is sure beginnin' to feel good to my hand . . . Mr. Parker?" He's gone! I spin around but he's not there, and then I see him, standing out by the separator, sipping water from the ladle, talking with Pa. Mr. Parker is pointing to me, then he slaps Pa on the shoulder, and they're both laughing. *Tuck-a-tuck-a-tuck-a-tuck-a-tuck-a*—she's running well, but pressure's down —time for a few more sticks of wood.

"You'll be ready for an outfit of your own, you betcha. That's what I was a-tellin' your pa." Mr. Parker climbs up beside me again, looking real pleased at the way his rig is running and that the water level in the glass is right where it ought to be. "That rack is the last of 'em, Peter, and then we'll be pullin' up stakes and moving on to the Estrems' place."

The sadness I felt earlier this morning comes back all of a sudden. If I was older, if I didn't have to go to school, then I could thrash all summer long and do all the neighbors' wheat.

"Now before we get too busy, I've got somethin' I'd like to give you . . . well, lend to you until we come back next year." Mr. Parker pulls off his gloves, tucks them under his arm, and digs down into a worn, grease-smudged canvas bag he carries with his bedroll. After some cursing and grumbling about how by now in the thrashin' season his life is scattered every which way, he comes up with two books, little books with brown covers and well-thumbed pages. "Here, Peter, I'd like you to have these," and he takes my hand, puts the books in them and closes my fingers around them. I don't know what to say, I'm so grateful and all. "Ya, sure, they're yours to read now." He motions to me to open the books and have a look at them.

Farm Engines and How to Run Them, the first one reads, *The Young Engineer's Guide.* I thumb through the pages, careful to turn each page from the upper right-hand corner, the way Miss Stavens taught us to do in school. There are beautiful little drawings showing the insides of a boiler, and the engine and all the different parts. Then I find a place where there are questions about how to run a steam engine and a thrashin' machine, and after each question the answer.

"You'll need to know all those answers when you take the examination for a steam engineer's license." Mr. Parker is looking over my shoulder. The other book says *Rough and Tumble Engineering,* on the cover, *A Book of Instructions for Operators of Farm Engines.* I try to say a thank you, not able to find the words, but Mr. Parker waves it off. "You don't have to thank me, young fellow. Truth to tell, it's not all that much, just a couple old books from an old engineer. But, by jippers, when you can help me run my rig next year and pass your examination so as to get your license, well now, that'll be thanks enough."

Mr. Parker reaches for the whistle cord and pulls down on it for a long time—we're done here and moving on to the next place. He looks around to make sure everyone's clear of the engine, and then he inches forward letting the belt slacken and drop to the ground. Pa and I shoulder the belt down off the big flywheel, roll it up and stow it on the separator. It seems like now I've done just about all there is to do, like a real thrasherman.

After a last lunch of lefse, and big pans of Ma's special coffee cake and pots and pots of coffee, the parade of bundle and grain wagons, water tank, and fuel wagon falls in line to leave. One by one, the men lay their forks in the wagons with a clatter, throw their bedrolls in, and climb in after them. Pa climbs up on a wagon seat as Ma and Aunt Mavis wave goodbye to everyone. It's his turn now to help thrash out the Estrems'. Ma and Aunt Mavis will go over later to help Tilda Estrem with the thrashers' supper.

When I reach up to Mr. Parker to shake hands goodbye, he just looks at me, smiling. "You ain't a-quittin' on us now are you? We've got a lot of wheat yet to thrash." He reaches down, grabs my hand and pulls me up onto the engine platform. "I need you to be my tankee and to be my fireman time to time. Let's see, I figure it'll take us this afternoon till supper, tomorrow and the better part of the next mornin' to thrash Estrem, so you'll be back to school come Monday mornin'. Ya, sure, you'll be a bit tuckered out, but back in plenty of time. Besides, you don't want to miss the square dance and ice cream social, now do you?"

The Storytellers

HANK BEEBE

MAVIS BROMAGHIM

MARY BROWER

HAL BUCKLIN

MARION CARTER

STEVEN DECATUR

GODFREY AND BETTY HUMANN

DON KUNITZ

TOM LAWRENCE

STEPHEN MARVIN

GERRY PARKER

JOHN SKARSTAD

REYNOLD AND HELEN WIK

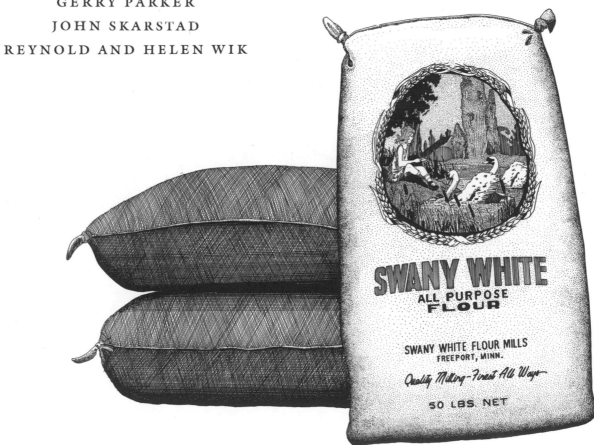

THRASHIN' TIME

was set in Galliard by DEKR Corporation,
Woburn, Massachusetts. Designed by Matthew
Carter and introduced in 1978 by the Mergenthaler
Linotype Company, Galliard is based on a type made by
Robert Granjon in the sixteenth century. It is the first type
of its genre to be designed exclusively for phototypesetting. A type
of solid weight, Galliard possesses the authentic sparkle that is lacking
in most current Garamonds. The italic is particularly felicitous
and reaches back to the feeling of the chancery style from
which Claude Garamond in his italic had departed.
Printed and bound by Friesens, Altona,
Manitoba, Canada.

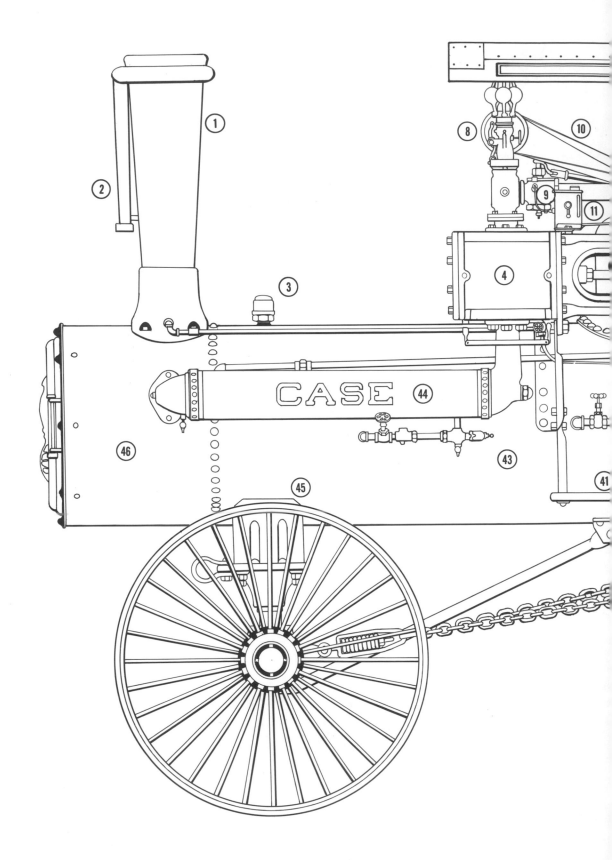

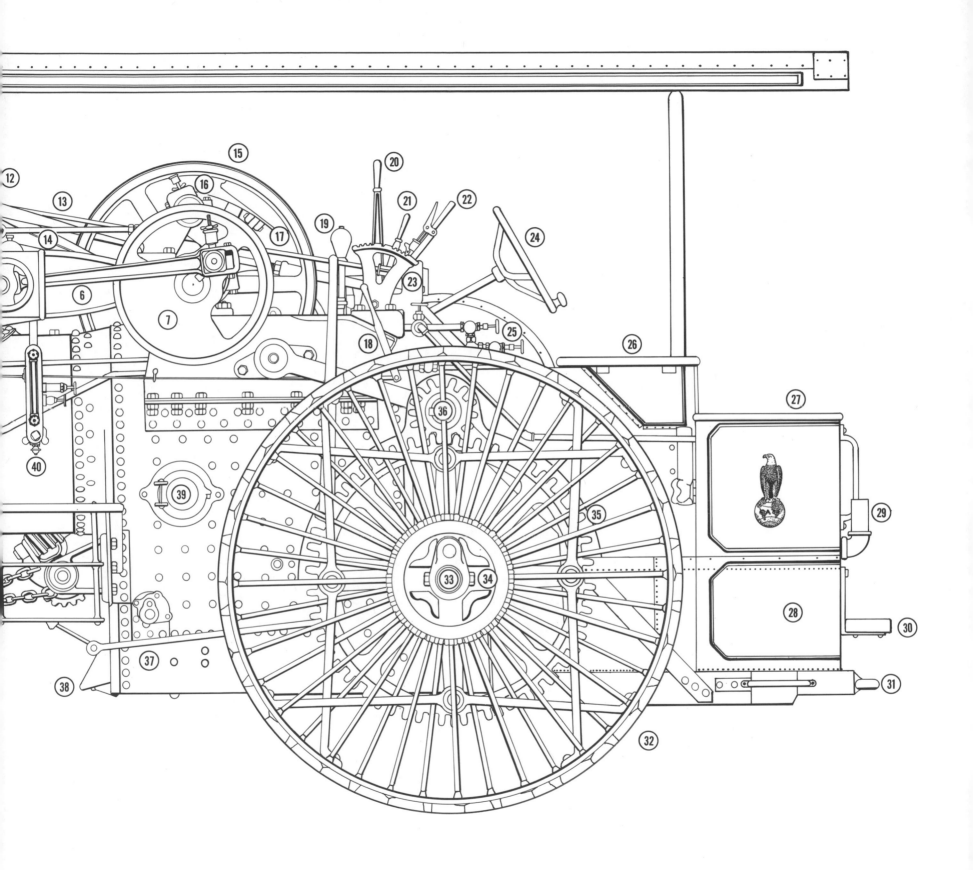